To my Ye

_____

With love from:

_____

Contents

Christian Media Publishers,
PO Box 4502, Durbanville, 7551
www.christianmediapublishing.com

Author: Ewald van Rensburg

Illustrations, Design & Layout: Lilani Brits

Publishing Project Manager: Noeline N Neumann

Reg No 2010/008573/07

No part of this publication may be reproduced
by any means – electronically or otherwise –
without the prior written permission of the publisher.

Text: Maranatha Publishing: Used by kind agreement.

Printed in Malaysia through PrettyInPress Productions.

First Editon, second printing, 2013
ISBN 978-1-920460-48-8

CMP-kids books have been developed with your child's
developmental phases and unique temperament in mind.
For a full explanation of the **unique temperament** and **developmental
phases** icons visit the CMP website **www.cmpublishing.co.za**

YesKids

Bible Stories
- about Love -

Kids saying YES! For Love

Written by Ewald van Rensburg
Illustrations by Lilani Brits

cmp
christian media publishing Kids

pointing children in the **right direction**

1. God provides food and water

(1 Kings 17)

Elijah was a man who talked to the Israelites about God. But King Ahab and the rest of the Israelites refused to listen to God's message.

So Elijah told King Ahab that it would not rain for a very long time, because he would not serve God. King Ahab decided to have Elijah killed. God told Elijah to hide away in a cave near a stream. There, Elijah had enough water to drink, but he had no food. He grew very hungry. So God sent crows with meat and bread in their beaks.

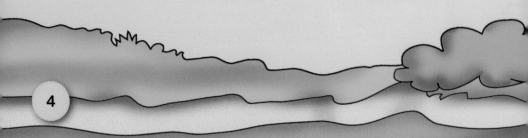

They brought food to Elijah twice a day, in the morning and in the evening.

Elijah knew that God would always care for him.

Come, let's pray together:

Dear Father, thank you that you always take care of me. Amen.

Always say thank you to Jesus that you have enough to eat and drink.

2. Nehemiah helps to make Jerusalem beautiful again

(Nehemiah 1 - 7)

Nehemiah was an Israelite. He was the cupbearer in the palace of the Persian king. This was an important job, because he had to taste everything served to the king, to make sure it wasn't poisoned.

Some of the Israelites who had returned to Jerusalem told him how terrible the city was looking. Even the city walls had been destroyed. God wanted Nehemiah to return to Jerusalem to help his people rebuild the city. Nehemiah loved God very much.

He realised he had to ask the Persian king to allow him to return to Jerusalem right away. He was rather scared about what the king would say, so he prayed before speaking to the king. The Lord answered his prayer. Nehemiah returned to Jerusalem. There they rebuilt the city beautifully, and promised to obey God forever.

Come, let's pray together:

Dear Father, help me always to obey you so I can also do wonderful things for you. Amen.

Nothing makes us happier than loving God.

3. Jonah disobeys God

(Jonah 2)

God told Jonah to go to the people of Nineveh and to tell them to stop sinning. He did not want to obey God so Jonah tried to run away from God. He sailed away on a boat. Jonah didn't realise that nobody can run away from God, because he sees everything.

Nineveh

Boat to Tarshish

Suddenly a storm blew up around Jonah's boat. Everyone on the boat was afraid. The sailors threw Jonah into the sea. God sent a large fish to save Jonah and it swallowed him up. Inside the fish's tummy Jonah told God that he was sorry he had run away.

The fish spat Jonah out onto the beach. Quickly Jonah went to Nineveh and did what God asked. He told the people to stop doing bad things. They said: "Lord, we are sorry," and God forgave them. This made Jonah angry, because he did not like the people of Nineveh. God said he loves everybody and that is why he forgave them.

Come, let's pray together:

Jesus, help me always to say sorry when I do something wrong. Amen.

Say you're sorry if you have done wrong. Jesus loves everyone, you too.

4. A father opens his arms
(Luke 15)

Jesus loved to tell stories. Here is one of his best ...

Once there was a good father, who loved his two sons very much.

One day the younger boy decided that he wanted to take his money and leave home.

The younger son travelled to a faraway country, where he wasted all his money When the money was all gone, he found a job looking after pigs. He was so hungry that he wanted to eat some of the pig's food.

Things became so tough for him that he decided to go home to his father. His father was hoping he would return. When he saw his son coming down the road, he ran to him and hugged him tight. His father was so happy to see him again that he gave him new clothes and organised a big party to celebrate him coming home.

Come, let's pray together:

Jesus, thank you that you told such wonderful stories, so we could learn how much you love us. Amen.

Our Heavenly Father
always loves us.

5. Jesus loves his friends
(John 13)

Jesus and his friends were sitting around the dinner table. Jesus saw that his friends' feet were dirty, because they had been walking in the streets all day in their sandals.

He took off his robe and tied a towel around his waist. Then he poured water into a basin. He began to wash his friends' feet, drying them with a towel afterwards. Peter was one of Jesus' best friends. Naturally he did not want Jesus as his leader, to wash his feet. "You will never wash my feet," he said.

Jesus answered, "If I don't wash your feet, you will not be part of me." So Peter allowed Jesus to wash his feet.

Jesus did this to show his friends how much he loved and cared for them.

Come, let's pray together:

Jesus, help me to always
love my friends.
Amen.

Remember to do special things for your friends.

Guidelines for parents

Faith Icon

The formation of faith is indeed unique to each child; there are however general characteristics which apply to all children. There are three main ways that children develop faith:

- Parents regularly reading the Bible, telling Bible and other faith based stories, praying together and doing faith building activities with their children (such as the ones found in this book).
- Children ask questions – parents need to take these questions seriously and answer them according to the child's level of understanding.
- Children follow the example of those caring for them.

Emotional intelligence icon

We experience emotions long before we learn the language to be able to express how we are feeling. Therefore it is important that children are taught to verbalise what they are feeling. Use the illustrations accompanying the stories and ask your child how they think the people or animals in the picture feel. This helps them become aware of their own emotions as well as those of others. It provides a learning opportunity where the child can learn appropriate words to express how they are feeling.

Reading icon

A wonderful world opens up for your child when they start learning to read. Enjoy every moment of this exciting adventure with your child. Let them sit on your lap where they can be comfortable and feel safe and secure. Open the book holding it so that you can both see the pages. Read clearly and with enthusiasm. As you know you can read the same story over and over. Point out where you are reading with your finger as you go along. This will help your child to begin to see the relationship between letters, sounds, words and their meaning. Encourage your child's attempts at reading – even of it sounds like gibberish.

Listening skills icon

Listening is an important learning and development skill. You can help develop this skill in your child by encouraging them to listen attentively, and understand what they are hearing. Let them look at the illustrations and then use their imagination to tell the story back to you in their own words. You can also encourage them to do this by asking questions relating to the story. Yet another way is to leave out words from a story the child knows well and let them fill in the missing words.

Vocabulary icon

Use every opportunity to build your child's vocabulary – it is a lifelong gift which you are giving to them. Start with everyday objects and people in the illustrations in books. Point at the picture, say the word, form a short sentence using the word. Repeat it again and then let your child say the word. Try to use the word in another context – if there is a tent in the picture you are looking at then say: we sleep in a tent when we go camping.

Numeracy skills icon

It is important for your child develop numeracy skills. Play simple games such as: "How many ducks are there in the picture? If we add two more ducks how many are there now? Then if three fly away? (use your fingers to illustrate this) How many are left? They also need to recognise the shape of numbers – cut large numbers from cardboard – let your child play with these – place the numbers in order forming a line from one to ten.